D1435699

THE GIRLS'
BOOK OF DREAMS

ARCTURUS

ARCTURUS

This edition published in 2011 by Arcturus Publishing Limited
26/27 Bickels Yard, 151–153 Bermondsey Street,
London SE1 3HA

Copyright © 2009 Arcturus Publishing Limited

All rights reserved. No part of this publication may be reproduced,
stored in a retrieval system, or transmitted, in any form or by any
means, electronic, mechanical, photocopying, recording or otherwise,
without prior written permission in accordance with the provisions of
the Copyright Act 1956 (as amended). Any person or persons who do
any unauthorised act in relation to this publication may be liable to
criminal prosecution and civil claims for damages.

ISBN: 978-1-84837-216-0
CH000570US

Author: Mandy Archer
Illustrations: Robyn Neild
Editor: Kate Overy
Supplier 03, Date 0911, Print run 1399

Printed in China

CONTENTS

Introduction

Are you a committed dreamer? Perhaps you find it easy to recount the funny, happy, out-of-this-world adventures that come to you while you sleep. Or maybe you're one of those people who honestly believe you don't ever dream. Whatever your story, this book is for you!

This guide offers you the key to unlocking your brain's sleeping messages, but only you can turn it. At the back of the book, there's a special dreamer's dictionary crammed full of suggestions about how to read the symbols you encounter during your sleep.

You're so much more fascinating than you realize! Now it's time to allow your dreams to reveal your amazing, creative inner self. Prepare to be truly inspired…

The Sweetness of Sleep

When you curl up under the covers and close your eyes at the end of the day, something amazing happens. Every night your sleeping mind becomes a theater, a stage bustling with an ever-changing program of dreams. What's more, YOU always take the starring role.

Everybody dreams, every single night. Although you may not remember a moment of it, your dream life is an important part of you. During our lives, we each sleep for a total of at least 20 years – so what does your mind do with all this time? This book will help you explore your dreams, learning how they express your most secret thoughts and feelings. Your inner self takes center stage every night while you are asleep – wouldn't you like to meet her?

Why do we dream?

Have you ever had a dream so heart-stoppingly vivid that it makes you sit bolt upright in bed? Maybe you've spent the early hours tossing and turning about an upcoming test, only to wake up convinced that you've already failed?

Sometimes dreams make such a strong impression on us that we have to pinch ourselves before we can fully understand that they weren't real. Other dreams can be hazy, but they leave us with a feeling that lingers on into the morning. So why do our brains go through this dreaming process every night?

DREAMER'S REAL-LIFE ACCOUNT:

"One night I dreamt I was running for my life. I don't know who or what was chasing me, but I had to get away. I scrambled into a pine forest. The trees were spiky and close together and it was difficult to climb over the rocks spread across the ground. I never did get caught, but when I woke up I was still panting from the effort of running all that way."

Ella

8

It seems unbelievable that the brain would put Ella through such an intense experience for no reason. There are all sorts of theories as to why we dream. Here are some of the most probable:

• Our brain might create dreams when it's trying to process outside interruptions that occur while we are asleep. This would explain how next door's barking dog could be worked into a dream sequence.

• Dreams give us the chance to act out our deepest desires or come to terms with our secret fears. Running through these scenarios in our dreams protects us from unwise actions in waking life.

• Dreamtime can be creative. Our dreams can seem jumbled and meaningless, but this state might be used to brainstorm new ideas.

• Could dreams simply be the brain doing its housework every night, to help our cluttered mind clean up and file away the events of the day?

How to use this guide

Although nobody is sure why we dream, many people agree that these subconscious experiences can teach us a lot about ourselves. Wouldn't it be fascinating to discover what your inner self is trying to tell you each night? This guide can't give you all the answers, but it does provide the questions you need to ask yourself to try to find some meaning in your sleeping life.

The thought of a dream-life may be something that has baffled you for ages, or it might even be something you've never really thought about before. Either way, next time you pull on your pajamas, take a second to think where your dreams might be about to lead you. As you get more in touch with your inner self, you'll even be able to start influencing and guiding your dreams to help you solve problems or understand important events in your life.

Dream Diary

This book will show you how to keep a dream diary and it offers tips on recalling your dreams. With practice, you'll also learn how to read the symbols hidden in your sleeping world and see how they reflect and enhance your daytime experiences.

Dream group

One thing's for sure – the more you analyze your dreams, the more helpful they will become. As you gain in confidence and skill, you can even try forming a dream group with your friends. Talking about your dreams with the people who know you best is another way of getting to understand what makes your inner self tick.

Dream Dictionary

At the back of this book you'll find a special dictionary, an A to Z with tips on decoding many of the themes and objects you might come across in your dreams. There are special entries concentrating on some of the most common things that might be on your mind each night – family, school, animals, love, money, and the future.

Good luck and sweet dreams!

Dreams arrive when your brain enters a phase called Rapid Eye Movement sleep – REM, for short. You can go through several episodes of REM sleep a night, each filled with its own amazing subconscious adventures. Even though scientists can't agree why we do it, one thing's for sure – dreams seem to offer a unique connection between our waking selves and our sleeping, subconscious mind.

In order to make the most of that connection, we all need to get enough sleep. But how much is enough? On average, teenagers need between eight and nine hours of shut-eye each and every night. That might sound like a lot, but each time you drop off, your brain has to travel through several stages of sleep before it is relaxed enough to move into a dream state.

In just one night...

Before you can get to the bottom of the dream that's been bugging you for ages, you need to understand the stages of sleep. Most nights your brain will go through four phases before entering REM sleep. The sleep cycle can last up to two hours! Once the four phases have been completed, your brain will start a new cycle, and repeat this pattern until morning.

REM – Really Exciting Moment!

The moment when you move into dream sleep is easy to spot. Suddenly your heart rate will increase and your eyes will begin to move noticeably beneath your eyelids. During REM sleep, your breathing quickens and your body flutters with activity.

This creative burst only lasts for a few minutes at first, but it gets repeated each time you go through your sleep cycle. Every time you experience REM, the episode gets longer and longer. It must be important, too – if you are woken during this dreaming phase, the next sleep cycle goes straight to REM until you make up the precious lost time.

THE STAGES OF SLEEP

1. As you start to drift off, your eye movements and brain waves gradually slow down. You can still be woken up easily, but your muscles have begun to loosen and relax.

2. During the second stage, your eye movements stop and your body's metabolism continues to slow down. Every so often your brain will experience rapid bursts of activity.

3. After 45 minutes, you're likely to have relaxed into a deep sleep. Your brain starts to create large 'delta' waves which move in slow curves, interspersed with faster movements. When you've reach this state, you become difficult to rouse. If someone does manage to wake you up, you'll feel confused and groggy.

4. When your brain only makes slow undulating delta waves, you've entered your deepest slumber. This important phase provides the good quality rest that you need to feel recharged and refreshed for the next day.

Getting enough of the good stuff – sleep!

Do your mom and dad give you a hard time for staying up late, then hiding under the covers next morning? Studies have shown that your body clock is different from those of adults and younger kids. Hormones released in your brain make it harder for you to fall asleep at night, which might explain why you sometimes need to catch up on your rest in the mornings.

TEN TIPS FOR A GOOD NIGHT'S REST:

1. *Set a regular bedtime*
This is golden rule number one. If your body gets into the habit of going to bed and waking up at around the same time, it will learn to read the signals and relax into deep sleep much more quickly.

2. *Exercise*
A good workout a few hours before bedtime is worth a hundred lullabies! Be active in the evenings as often as you can.

3. *Avoid caffeine*
Cola drinks and coffee are full of stimulants that wreak havoc with your body's rhythms. Avoid them from mid-afternoon.

4. *Keep the lights low*
Your brain is programed to sleep during darkness. Help it out by turning down the lights before you go to bed.

5. Relax your mind
Help yourself unwind by establishing a pampering bedtime routine.
Have a bubble bath, turn on some calming music and potter
around in your bedroom for an hour or so.

6. Turn off the TV/games console/laptop/cellphone…
Computer games and spooky movies are just the sort of things to
send adrenalin rushing around your body. Switch off and log out
at least two hours before bedtime.

7. Set the scene
Make sure your bedroom is a quiet and comfortable place, where
you can sleep soundly. Turn the heating down, then layer up with
blankets until the temperature feels just right.

8. Cut out the cat naps
Occasionally you might get so sleepy your brain will demand a
shutdown to recuperate. The odd nap is fine, but try to limit it to half
an hour so that you are still tired when bedtime comes around.

9. Find the amount of sleep that's right for you
Experiment with different bedtimes until you find the hour that
allows you to wake up with a spring in your step.

10. Wake up with a zing!
When the alarm goes off, avoid snooze-mode! Force yourself to
flick on the light and pull open the drapes straight away. A dose
of bright light tells your body that it's time to get up.

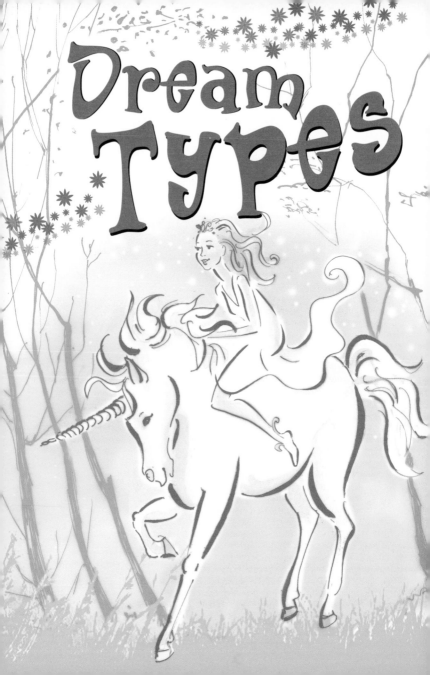

Dreams come in many curious shapes and forms. While some may just seem to be flights of fancy designed to help us relax and unwind, others appear to have a more practical purpose. Some lead us to answers we've been searching for for ages, while others remind us of important things that need attention from our waking selves.

Most dreamers soon learn to organize their dreams into certain key types, in the same way that they'd sort out and file the music on an MP3 player. Labeling dreams like this helps us get to the heart of their meaning more quickly. Once you've established the purpose of your dream, you can start to look at the detail with expert and perceptive eyes.

Chilling out

As you nod off into your first sleep cycle of the night, the chances are that you'll experience a "processing dream." When this happens, your brain throws up one or two images and sequences, repeating them again and again.

Processing dreams aren't loaded with meaning – they're just your mind's way of relaxing and dealing with the events of the day. These dreams are often quickly forgotten once you wake up.

DREAMER'S REAL-LIFE ACCOUNT:

"Last week we put on our school's annual production. I'm not the sort of person to get up on stage, but this year my friends roped me into singing in the chorus. There were tons of songs and I found it quite tricky to remember all the words — but I managed to get through it (just!). When I went to bed after the show I had the strangest dream. I was auditioning in a reality TV show, singing a number from the school musical! It was weird, I never made it past the second verse without looping back and starting again."

Gaby

Sort and warn

When you've got a tricky problem to sort out, sometimes your subconscious steps in to help. In "problem-solving" dreams, your inner self draws you into scenarios that can point you towards a decision, or warn you against something that's been on your mind during waking hours.

A problem-solving dream can take a little more interpretation than a straightforward processing one. Sometimes the meaning hides behind the story of your dream, or is suggested in the scenarios or objects that come up. On other mornings you might just wake up with an inexplicable feeling or urge to do something that suddenly feels instinctive and right.

THINK ABOUT IT

It's worth thinking through a problem-solving dream, as it could unlock an issue that has been troubling you for some time. We are all subject to social worries and pressures during our daily lives, but your sleeping self is free to strip these away and get to the heart of the matter.

All in the mind

Even the most confident über-babe in town can be plagued by insecurities about her appearance or popularity. Coping with school, relationships and parents is draining, and if you're unlucky enough to have something bad happen on top of all that you're a good candidate for a "psychological dream."

These dreams occur when your life seems out of balance. Your inner self will try to help you overcome your fears and emotions by presenting you with a phobia, or a nightmare, to make its point.

DREAMER'S REAL-LIFE ACCOUNT:

"My biggest cringe was getting food stuck in my dental braces. One summer, I was so upset I'd pretty much stopped going out. I dreamt that my teeth got wedged with bits of ham while I was eating a sandwich in the school canteen! But it was alright — my friend handed me a mirror and I sorted them out. Even though it was just a dream, I stopped worrying about the braces and got on with enjoying my vacation."

Jemma

Fantastic fantasies

"Wish fulfilment" dreams have got to be the nicest sleeping experiences of all! These flights of fancy allow your brain to be as creative as it desires, imagining yourself in the scenarios you've secretly wished and hoped for during waking hours.

The sky's the limit during these nocturnal adventures – your subconscious could see you married to your pop idol, strutting your stuff on the catwalk or chilling out on a luxury desert island!

CHASE YOUR DREAMS

As well as being pleasurable, wish fulfilment dreams can provide you with all kinds of unexpected ideas and inspiration. By placing you firmly center stage, they are tremendous confidence boosters. Your inner self knows just how to give you the right dream at the right time, offering the encouragement you need to go for something that really matters.

Looking ahead

Can we really see the future before it happens? People who have been affected by a "precognitive dream" swear that this is true. Dreams that offer predictions aren't always filled with end-of-the-world revelations or lottery tips, although they might foretell something smaller or closer to home.

Precognitive dreams are rare, but they often seem to have an other-worldly feel to them. Dreamers often talk about unusual lighting, muffled speech or a setting that seems slightly unfamiliar or distorted.

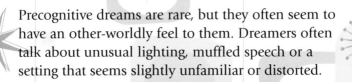

PAUSE AND REWIND

When our brain plays the same sequence over and over again, we are experiencing a "recurring dream." When this happens, our mind's eye shows us the same people and places again and again, repeating conversations like a stuck record. Could it be that our inner self has a message so important that it replays it until we sit up and listen? Recurring dreams should be listened to closely, as subtle developments in the dream could indicate that things have changed in the real world.

Double dreams

Have you ever got up in the morning, raced to the bathroom and started to dress before realizing that you have been dreaming all along? "False awakenings" happen when you believe you have woken up, but are actually still asleep.

These dreams often focus on everyday routines that are burnt onto your memory. As well as being over-used in soaps and horror movies, these "dreams within a dream" are usually very convincing and rather disorientating.

SLEEPWALKING

As we grow up, we tend to sleepwalk less and less, but some adults do still try to act out their dreams when they sleep at night. Sleepwalking is more common when you're under a lot of pressure at school or at home and is often accompanied by sleeptalking. This night-time activity can be harmless and rather funny, but if you're worried about it, you could ask your mom or dad to make an appointment with your doctor to put your mind at rest. Don't lose any sleep over it!

Capturing Dreams

Have you ever tried that beat-the-alarm-clock trick? As you drift off to sleep, gently tap your head on the pillow the right number of times to match the hour you want to wake up the next morning. For example, try seven taps for seven o'clock. Most people who give this a shot open their eyes just before seven o'clock – proving what can be achieved when you set your mind to something.

It's exactly the same scenario when it comes to tracking your dreams. You might think that you hardly ever remember what goes on in your imagination while you sleep, but you can change that if you want to. If you ask your inner self to make your dreams a priority, you'll gradually be able to piece together more and more of the jigsaw. Capturing your dreams is the first step on the amazing learning journey of getting in touch with your inner self.

Why it's worth it

Life can be crazily busy these days. Our waking hours are filled with socializing, chores, travel and clubs – and that's just the weekends! But if you forget your dreams each morning you could miss out on some valuable advice and inspiration.

World famous dreamers

Writers, musicians, inventors, actors – all kinds of famous people have believed in the power of dreams. Some have even used their visions to solve problems and make discoveries that have rocked the world. Here are three of the best:

1. Mary Shelley

Shelley wrote the chilling gothic novel *Frankenstein* after being troubled by a vivid nightmare. Since 1818, the book has been turned into countless stage plays and movies.

2. Robert Louis Stevenson

Stevenson wrote the famous story of *Dr Jekyll and Mr Hyde* after he dreamt key elements of the plot. He also claimed he was able to revisit storylines in his dreams.

3. Paul McCartney

The ex-Beatles singer/songwriter came up with the melody for *Yesterday* after hearing it being played in a dream. The song went on to become the most covered track of all time.

The Hollywood hit list

Even the biggest names in LA have talked about the powerful motifs that appear in their dreams. It's believed that some have even consulted professional interpreters in a bid to unravel their meanings.

HOLLYWOOD DREAM GIRLS

- Tyra Banks
- Rhianna
- Hallé Berry
- Madonna
- Christina Aguilera
- Gwyneth Paltrow

Take note!

Something as simple as a notebook on your bedside table can get you into the habit of tracking your own dreamlife. Often we are so busy pleasing other people and fitting in, we forget to be kind to ourselves.

Your inner self only thinks about you. It's like having a secret friend who is always there to help you through tough times and steer you towards exciting new opportunities. The more attuned you become to your dreamlife, the more you'll be able to deal with the trials and tribulations of the real world.

Where to start

Are you the kind of person who wouldn't wake up even if there was a rave going on in your bedroom? If so, you probably have trouble recalling what happened during the eight hours that you were sleeping each night.

Don't panic! There are all sorts of things you can do to record these fleeting memories before they disappear forever. Even the deepest sleeper can learn to track her dreams. It just takes practice and some discipline.

RULES FOR TOP-NOTCH NOTE-TAKING

• Write down exactly what happened in your dream – don't be tempted to edit yourself.

• Think of how all five senses were affected – sight, smell, touch, hearing and even taste.

• Don't make any snap judgements about what you've written.

• Jot down how you felt when you woke up. Were you happy, sad, confused or relieved?

Top dream-tracking tips

All of this might seem like a bit of an effort at first, but these simple steps will really help you keep track of your dreams. Then you'll be able to decode your dream messages and learn what they mean.

1. Before you go to sleep, have a plain notepad and pen ready. Ask your mind to remember what is going to happen in your dreams. Say the request out loud several times and keep it in your head as you close your eyes.

2. Stick a note on your bedside table and write the words "Describe your dream" in big letters so it's the first thing you see when you wake up.

3. If you use an alarm clock, set it to a chime or buzzer rather than the radio. The chatter of voices or pop tunes will distract you as you come round. Make sure you can turn your alarm off quickly and easily.

4. When you wake up, try to stay as still as possible. Don't move until you've thought back to the night before and recited as many memories you can. Keep your mind focussed and don't be distracted by any morning hustle and bustle outside your bedroom door.

Your dream journal

Now that you're starting to capture more and more of your dreams, it is time to start making a dream journal. This document will become your most valuable tool in the quest to discover your inner self – an amazing resource packed with fascinating evidence about you and your deepest feelings.

Creating a dream journal is the perfect way to show how serious you are about interpreting your dreams and getting to know your inner self. It's also a fun, creative project that's great to work on with your best friend after school or at the weekend!

When you've found a notebook you like, it's time to get customizing! Use glitter, ribbon, photos and gift wrap to transform the pad into a journal that reflects you in every way. Use your favorite colors, find a special pen to write with and decorate the cover until you've made something that you're really proud of. Each time you record a dream, take your rough notes and transcribe them neatly on a new page in your journal.

Here is a blank template from a dream journal to help you get started:

Dream title: ....

Date: ....

Time: ....

Theme: ....

Setting: ....

Lighting and weather: ....

Emotions: ....

Activity: ....

Characters: ....

My account: ....

....

....

....

How I felt when I woke up: ....

....

....

Possible meaning: ....

....

Sketches:

Reading Your Dreams

Flicking through a dream journal can make for some seriously weird reading. Accounts of talking animals, flying people and crazy encounters in random places can make your subconscious sound like it is, quite frankly, nuts.

It's not easy to reach back into your sleeping life and pull out meaningful messages. Interpreting your dreams requires skill, imagination and an open mind. At night your subconscious speaks to you through a series of pictures. When you study your dreams, you need to look at the symbols and codes hidden in the things you see.

Dreams are complex and multi-faceted, just like you. Is your inner self trying to tell you two or more things at once? Remember that there is rarely only one right answer.

Making connections

Most of your dreams can't be taken literally. They are an intense bundle of ideas and images – the output of the staggeringly intricate human brain. Experts aren't able to unearth a dream's secrets for you; instead, you have to search inside yourself to find out what you think your subconscious might be saying.

Objects, people and places mean different things to different people. A dreamer's dictionary (like the one on page 74) can suggest definitions, but it certainly doesn't have all the answers.

DEEPER MEANING

Mia for example, once dreamt that she was sitting by a pool, looking down at a shiny green frog. Frogs are said to represent inner beauty and even transformation, but Mia knew that couldn't be true for her. Ever since a frog had leapt over her foot as a small girl, she had been scared stiff of the ribbety, slimy creatures. Mia could see that her dream was actually about being brave and facing her fears.

Step back in time

When it comes to rustling up new dreams, your brain is not short of material. It has a lifetime's worth of memories tucked away in its archive, ready to pull out at a moment's notice.

When people from your past are blended with the here and now in your dreams, it can be both confusing and at times upsetting. The thing to remember is that there is a connection between your old and recent memories that your inner self is trying to point out to you.

Stand back and try to forget about all the details from your dream for a moment. Instead, ask yourself how you felt. Could emotions you felt in the past be similar to the ones you're feeling now?

Perhaps you learnt a life lesson the first time round that is worth remembering as you move forward. If the answer doesn't become clear, don't worry. Your sleeping mind will keep presenting the information to you in different ways until it gets the message through.

Literal or symbolic?

Even short processing dreams can have several layers of meaning. Imagine that you are feeling hurt after being blanked by a friend at the shopping center. The next night in bed you might dream that she is walking away from you, her silhouette disappearing into the darkness. When you wake up you might feel sad to think that you've lost a good friendship, but could there be another interpretation?

Darkness can signify sadness or the unknown. Instead of turning her back on you, your pal might actually be going through a bad or lonely time herself that is making her seem unfriendly or disinterested. Perhaps your subconscious is asking you to be patient and forgive the upsetting encounter you had in the mall.

CRACK THE CODE

When it comes to choosing the right dream interpretation, you act as the filter. It's up to you to decide what elements in your dream match your waking experiences and which are hidden clues or symbols that need to be decoded further.

DREAMER'S REAL-LIFE ACCOUNT:

"Last term I had a strange recurring dream. Most nights I imagined that I was cycling through a complicated one-way system, a long way from home. At first I thought that this just had something to do with my new bike. It wasn't until I noticed that all the traffic lights were fixed on green, that the true meaning dawned on me. For days I had been wishing I could call up my dad. After my parents got divorced he had moved away to live with his new girlfriend in the city. Each time I tried talk to my mom about my feelings she had got so upset that I'd just let the subject drop. I hadn't seen my dad since he'd given me the bike for my birthday. I'm convinced that the green lights were my subconscious trying to tell me that it was OK to go ahead and pick up the phone. Once I'd chatted to him I felt miles better and my mom didn't mind at all."

Megan

The power of words

You are so much cleverer than you think you are. During waking hours, we only use a small proportion of our brains to reason, interact and function. When we are asleep, other areas of our intellect come alive, dredging up information that we could never access while we are conscious.

As well as presenting you with challenging pictures and scenarios, your inner self is a master of word play. Sometimes its messages to you are hidden in puns and metaphors, clues that need to be unpicked and deciphered.

WHAT'S IN A PUN?

Puns are often funny. When someone makes a pun they use words that sound similar but have clearly different meanings. Your brain is very skillful at slotting puns into your dreams. Look back through your journals and think how the words you have written down could be interpreted in a different way.

Word play

If you have dreamt of sailing across a lake, for example, your subconscious could also be suggesting that you are going to "sail" through an upcoming ballet or school exam. A dream placing you in an automobile with failing brakes could be trying to tell you it's time to put the "brakes" on a new project or relationship in your waking life.

If you dream about a pig, you inner self might be trying to indicate that you are being greedy about something. An encounter with a wizard, however, could be suggesting something more subtle. Do you have a skill or talent that you aren't making the most of? Place the wizard in the context of your dream and look for signposts. Is your inner self telling you that you're magic at soccer, writing or making people laugh?

MAD METAPHORS

When your subconscious speaks to you in metaphor, it uses a familiar image or word to suggest a different meaning altogether. Sometimes the comparison is obvious, but other times it's not so clear.

Trust your feelings

Each time you capture your dreams, and fill in your dream diary, you get to know yourself a little better. The entries might be a jumble of events, people, symbols and messages but this is fine!

By now you will have realized that the scenes you encounter during your sleep can have several meanings – so how do you go about deciding which interpretation is the right one?

The answer is simple – follow your heart. The way that you feel about a dream is as important as the detail and imagery you experience. If you wake up with butterflies in your stomach, look at the sign that your inner self is trying to show you. Your subconscious is not tied by rules and doesn't care what other people think of it. So your instinctive reaction is the right one. Sometimes your gut feelings can help you to resolve situations in your waking life.

DREAMER'S REAL-LIFE ACCOUNT:

"The other night I dreamt that I was at a sleepover with all my best friends. I can remember clearly that I was wearing a new pair of green pajamas. Everybody was laughing at a story my friend Leah was telling and we were all tucking into snacks and drinks. It seemed like a great party, but when I woke up I couldn't understand why I felt so cross. When I thought about it again at school, I realized that although Leah was a brilliant laugh, I sometimes felt jealous of all the attention she got. I'd never admitted this to anyone before, least of all myself! Accepting those feelings helped me get over it and move on."

Amy

Look inside yourself

Did you know that babies spend about two-thirds of their sleep in the REM phase? As we grow older, the amount of dream time we experience decreases, with most adults only dreaming for one-fifth of their sleep cycle. It seems certain that dreaming plays a key role in helping our brains grow and develop. So it makes sense that prioritizing your dream life can help you make the most of your potential in all sorts of unexpected ways.

Sometimes you can feel like a spectator of your dreams. Even if you are just watching from the sidelines, you can learn a lot about yourself by taking note of what you do and how you behave.

SEARCH YOUR JOURNAL FOR CLUES

Go back through your dream journal and look at how your inner self thinks and acts. Is she like you or does she behave completely differently? Perhaps your dream self is the sort of person you would like to be if you had the courage. Alternatively she could be holding parts of your character you are not so proud of up to the light.

It's all about me

Go through the checklist below and ask yourself the following questions. Building up a picture of your dream self can help you make positive changes to your life or learn to love yourself a bit better.

1. Do I look the same as normal, or am I older, younger or do I have a different body shape/clothes?

2. Am I speaking in my dreams and does my voice sound like it usually does?

3. Do I tend to react as I would during my waking life, or am I more or less confrontational?

4. Do I have extra skills or abilities that I don't normally have?

5. Am I doing things that I have never tried before?

6. Am I proud of my behavior or am I being deceitful or mean?

7. Am I leading the action in my dream or do I seem to be a victim or a bystander?

Familiar Dreams

Ever dreamt that you were running away from someone sinister, only to find that you were moving in slow motion? Most of us will be able to recognize the terrible feeling of having our legs rooted to the spot, while everybody around us dashes to safety. This is just one of a handful of dreams we all experience at one time or another, no matter how old we are or where we come from. Maybe it's a sign that, inside, our hopes and fears aren't that different after all.

What makes your interpretation unique is finding out how your version of a common dream varies from everyone else's. Although you may share similar problems to your friends, the details of your particular dream will lead you to the solution that's right for you.

Flying

Flying in your sleep is often described as a "lucid" type of dream – an experience where you are aware that you are dreaming while the adventure is unfolding (see pages 66–7). Most teens say that flying dreams are thrilling, happy and uplifting. As you soar over the countryside, your inner self feels a rush of freedom, and you feel as though you can do anything. Flying dreams are common just before a change is due, often appearing at times when you're contemplating exciting things in the future.

Falling

Falling dreams can leave you feeling panicky and agitated. As you tumble through the air, your inner self is trying to highlight an area of your life that is causing you anxiety. If you are pushed over the edge of something in your dream, the sense of being out of control can be even stronger. In these dreams, your inner self knows that forcing you to look at an issue that troubles you is the best way of making you deal with it. There's a myth that you will die if you don't wake up before you hit the ground – don't believe a word of it. Falling dreams are really very common and dreamers always live to tell the tale!

Being chased

Being pursued is another classic anxiety dream. When you're feeling small and intimidated, running is a natural instinct. It takes guts, but the best way to resolve a chase dream is to stand your ground and confront your pursuer. What is this creature who is chasing you and why won't it leave you alone? Although it may look extremely threatening, the attacker is often just a part of yourself. When you face the things that they are trying to show you, the dreams usually disappear.

Losing things

When a big change happens in your life, it's quite normal to dream about losing precious objects, such as your purse or keys. Changing schools, moving house, or a new addition to the family can be unsettling for a while, even if you've looked forward to the change for months. Your friends, family and surroundings all help define who you are, so it's natural to express a concern about losing part of your identity at these times. Losing objects in your dream can make you feel uncomfortable for a while, but once you accept that the dream might reflect real life, you'll be free to move on.

Failing exams

Ask your friends to take a vote on who's not had this one! All of us at sometime or another will have a dream where we are doing hideously at some kind of exam or test. Often the circumstances are really gruelling and embarrassing – perhaps you haven't revised or even attended the classes! In other dreams you might turn up late or with a pen that won't work. Exam dreams tend to be literal in their meaning, suggesting that you are feeling under-prepared and lacking in confidence about an upcoming challenge. Use it as a 'heads up' and think about how you can put yourself back in control.

Being seen naked

Most people who experience this cringeworthy dream find it horrendously embarrassing! Often you are going about a normal routine such as shopping or sitting in class when the awful truth dawns that you are the only person without any clothes on. Your inner self is sending you a clear message – something in your waking life is making you feel vulnerable and unprotected. The interesting thing is that in most dreams, nobody even bats an eye about your nudity. This indicates that your fears aren't grounded and there's no need to feel insecure.

Wobbly teeth

If you've had a dream about your teeth wobbling, crumbling or falling out, you'll probably be able to remember very clearly how disturbing and uncomfortable it made you feel. Our teeth are central to our sense of image – on show whenever we smile or say 'hello'. Losing teeth can suggest that you are feeling insecure about your looks or how you present yourself to others. The next time you wake up from a dream like this, take a look at yourself in the mirror. Examining your teeth and realizing that they are all in place should reassure you that these worries aren't based on the real, beautiful you.

Monsters

Terrifying beasts, witches and werewolves always have a symbolic meaning in dreams. Your subconscious personifies the scary side of someone that has unnerved you during the day by turning them into a monster. Often these frightening creatures are people that are very familiar to you, such as teachers or your parents. Adults can make us feel anxious when they shout or get angry, so this dream could be our way of working through our reaction to this behavior.

Taking Control of Your Dreams

Once you've got a good thing going on with your inner self, it's time to start asking a few questions of your own. If there is a specific problem troubling you, ask your subconscious to step in and shed some light on it. Your waking and sleeping selves make a great team; the more they co-operate, the more helpful your dreams will become. As your interpretation skills grow, you can even learn how to revisit certain dreams and try to influence their outcomes.

Learning to read the language of dreams is sure to lead you on a fascinating journey of self-discovery. Suddenly the random pictures and voices that dance across your sleeping mind can give you valuable insights about yourself, helping you to take control of your waking and sleeping minds, to live a healthier, happier life.

Dream incubation

Now that you are tracking your dreams and learning to interpret what they might tell you about yourself, it's time to go one step further. Focused dreamers can actually influence their dreams, using their dream-time to answer questions that are troubling them or to explore issues that they're grappling with during waking hours. Taking charge of your dreams is called "dream incubation." It takes practice, but if you work on it, anybody can do it.

Dream incubation is the art of strengthening the connection between your waking mind and your subconscious. Although dreams can be strange, confused or just plain crazy, we already know that they are a response to the experiences you've had during the day. Amidst the confusion are real insights and judgements that can help us in all sorts of ways. When you incubate your dreams, you are helping to focus your mind in a positive way.

Do you have a question that has been bugging you for days? Perhaps you're agonizing over a decision about your best friend, school or a new romance. Dream incubation can offer you a helping hand – once you've learnt the technique, you'll be amazed at how responsive your inner self can be!

Using dream power the right way

Guiding your dreams through dream incubation is a subtle skill. To learn the most from your subconscious you need to ask the right questions. Use this five-point plan to steer your sleeping mind towards an issue that is important to you.

1. Consider your question seriously. Focus on things in your life that you really care about. Don't waste time on the trivial stuff.

2. Avoid questions that are too vague and ones that require only a "yes" or "no" answer.

3. Write your question down on a piece of paper, so that it stays in your mind during the day.

4. Keep focused on the issue you need help with. Take comfort in the knowledge that while you dream, your subconscious should shed some light on your emotions during the night.

5. Be prepared to listen to the answer. Your dream will show you the truth about your feelings, even if it's hard to accept.

Dream re-entry

If you have a dream that keeps bugging you long after you have woken up, "dream re-entry" might help. This technique allows you to go back into a dream to settle unfinished business or answer a question. Don't attempt "dream re-entry" with a nightmare though – it's best to leave them alone!

The tips below will show you how to set all the right conditions for re-entry, but don't be disappointed if it doesn't work straightaway.

• As you prepare for sleep, try to recall the setting of your original dream. Where were you?

• Decide how you would like to change the ending of your dream this time around. Repeat this as you fall asleep, so that it stays in the front of your mind.

• As soon as you recognize your dream unfolding, step forward and challenge what happened last time. Always try to end your dream in a positive, happy way.

• When you wake up, scribble the key points in your note pad. Include as much detail as you can so that you can analyze it later.

DREAMER'S REAL-LIFE ACCOUNT:

"One night I had a terrible dream about my hamster, Buttercup. I was stroking her when she suddenly bared her teeth and tried to bite my neck. I panicked and pushed her away. When I woke up I felt so shaky I could hardly bear to look over at her cage. I've had Buttercup since I was nine and she hasn't even nipped me once. I didn't want to see Buttercup like that again, but I decided that I had to go back into my dream and confront her. It took a few nights of trying, but eventually I made it. She started to attack me again, so I wrapped her in my bedspread until she calmed down. Within seconds she was gentle again and I felt that I could leave. My mom said the nightmare might have been brought on by my move to high school. I felt scared about going to a new place that might not be as friendly. Facing up to Buttercup showed me that there was nothing to be scared of after all."

Rachelle

The Mystics of
Dreaming

Wise people, gurus and thinkers have always been intrigued by dreams. The adventures that unfold during our sleep can be so convincing, some have found it hard to believe that they can just be a mere illusion.We already know that dreams are still largely unexplained by science. We have also learnt that our brains are immensely powerful organs with an infinite capacity for creating new ideas.

What if our sleeping minds were able to transcend the limits of our waking selves and do things we wouldn't normally think possible? If you believe that there could be more to our dream-lives than a jumble of unconscious ideas, you are ready to explore the mystical side of dreaming.

Shared dreams

Remember the saying "a problem shared is a problem halved?" When you can't get to grips with the message embedded in your dreams, talking it through with someone you trust can shed a whole new light on things.

The friends who know you best can often spot symbols and connections that you might find difficult to notice or understand for yourself. The more you open up and share your dreams with your best friends, the more you could learn about your dream life and your inner self.

If you and your friends love to chat about anything and everything, why not suggest setting up a dream group? Now that they've probably heard how you've been developing your dream skills, they're bound to want to join in! The best news is that a dream group is a fantastic way of getting to know your pals inside and out.

Trust each other

A dream group needs to be run on trust. Before meeting up, friends should promise to keep each other's secrets no matter what, and to take the session seriously. You have to dig deep to get to know your inner self, so your friends must be prepared to listen carefully – that means no laughing at each other and no interrupting when someone is trying to share their dreaming experiences.

Once your group is working well together, you'll be ready to take your dream investigations one step farther.

Focused friends that are really in tune with each other can sometimes learn to incubate the same dream. There have even been cases of people meeting each other in their dreams and reporting the same story back to the group at the next meeting. Dream telepathy is even more astounding, as it allows a person to communicate a specific message to the other group members just by focussing his or her dreams in the right direction.

Forming a dream group

A dream group isn't hard to set up, but it does require a leader. One of you needs to "chair" the meetings – inviting people to come forward to share their dreams and encouraging the others to ask questions.

No one should be bossed around or asked to tell the group anything she feels uncomfortable about sharing. Instead the atmosphere should be relaxed, friendly and open.

Dream destination

Find a quiet place to meet up, such as a bedroom, and then make diary dates to meet up at a regular time every couple of weeks. When all your friends have arrived, ask everyone to sit in a circle and turn down the lights. Hold each other's hands and close your eyes for a few moments, until the atmosphere is calm and you're all ready to listen very carefully to each other.

When you sense that everybody is completely relaxed, ask the first person to tell you about her dream. Although it is tempting to shout out meanings, ask everyone to wait until the dreamer has had her say.

You decide

No matter how sure you are about the messages in someone else's dream, nobody in the group should tell another member what her dream is about. If it feels right, offer some sensitive suggestions, but remember that only the dreamer can ultimately decide what her inner self is trying to say to her.

DREAMER'S REAL-LIFE ACCOUNT:

"Our first dream group meeting was totally chaotic. All my friends were so excited, no one could get a word in edgeways! Although I knew the most about reading dreams, I just felt too shy to keep everyone in line. In the end my friend Sunita took the lead. She got everybody to agree a few things up front. The biggest one was that no one should be forced to tell anything if they didn't want to – no pressure! After we sorted the rules and put Sunny in charge, it went brilliantly! I've learnt loads about myself and we all feel that's there's a special bond of friendship between the members of the group."

Georgia

Joint dream incubation

When you and your friends have got into the habit of meeting regularly, you might want to experiment with incubating a dream together. At the end of a session, suggest that the whole group meets up in your dreams. Decide on a night during the following week that you're all going to try to meet.

Find a location that everybody knows, so that when you all go to bed on that evening you'll have no trouble visualizing the setting. When that night comes, you might find you have a completely different dream experience, but write down exactly what happens anyway, even if it seems unrelated. When you meet up with the other members of your dream group, share your experiences and see how everyone's accounts tally up!

Make magic happen

When you all get onto the same wavelength, it's amazing what a dream group can achieve. You might be surprised by the positive outcomes that suddenly present themselves, as if by magic! It's fun to try out dream incubation with your friends, but even if you don't succeed in having the same dream, it's no big deal! Supporting the other members of your dream group is the most important thing.

Dream telepathy

Some ambitious dreamers have even tried to use the power of their subconscious to communicate messages to each other, even though they might be sleeping in bedrooms miles apart!

Nobody has proved whether dream telepathy is possible, but it's a simple and exciting thing to try with the other members of your dream group.

Ask someone in the group to incubate a dream about a specific possession for as many nights as she can. It is important that she doesn't mention the name of the possession to anyone in the group. The others should be instructed to go to bed each evening with an open mind.

When it's time to report back on the symbols and objects they have encountered, take care to listen to all the details. Often dreamers are surprised by the accuracy of the answers.

Lucid dreaming

It can be pretty tough to stay awake sometimes! Whether you're sitting in the back of the automobile during a long journey or snuggled on the sofa in front of a DVD, it's hard to resist sleep when your eyelids start to get heavy.

These impromptu naps are sometimes worth giving in to – if you're lucky, you might even get to experience a "lucid dream."

Unforgettable

In a lucid dream, your mind has drifted into its usual dream state, but your conscious self is present and aware of what's going on. These rare dreams often take place when you are napping, floating halfway between your waking and sleeping states.

Knowing that you are dreaming gives you the power to direct the action, which means you can do anything or go anywhere you want to! Being able to control what you do in your dream life is a rare and amazing power. Most lucid dreamers say that the experience is unforgettable.

Live the dream

The possibility of lucid dreaming proves that we always have control over our own destiny. Even when we are asleep, we have the power to connect with our inner selves and resolve problems in the way we think is best.

Despite this, it's important to keep in touch with what is real and what is not real in our lives. The mystical power of dreams is an enormous realm that we are only just starting to map, but its most significant purpose is to enhance and illuminate our waking experiences.

In your dream world anything is possible – literally. We mentioned earlier that most flying dreams are lucid (see page 48), but in this state you are free from all the restrictions of every day life, including gravity! So many people have now testified to being lucid dreamers, scientists agree that this phenomenon must be real.

putting
Worries to
Rest

Your bed should be a cosy, comfortable, quiet place – your own personal retreat. Very occasionally, however, your bedroom can become a spooky or unsettling domain where the dreams you experience leave you feeling frightened, troubled and upset.

Nightmares and negative dreams are seldom literal. Seeing these difficult sleep times as a challenge will help you to understand why they happen and may bring you some peace of mind. Once you hold a light up to these dark episodes, you'll see why your inner self is trying to grab your attention, and you'll learn to put worries to rest.

Nightmares

Bad dreams can be terrifying, shocking and upsetting. The important thing to remember is that they are not real. Nobody should underestimate how frightened a nightmare can make you feel – especially a recurring dream that plagues you for nights on end.

Troubled nights can leave you feeling tired, down and even scared about going to bed. To make things worse, evidence seems to suggest that nightmares are much more common during your childhood and teenage years.

Do not fear

The good news is that there are lots of things you can do to tackle these bad dreams. Nightmares are the product of your subconscious brain holding up your fears and insecurities and waving them in your face for you to deal with. Sometimes, though, they can be triggered by something external, such as a scary story, over-tiredness or even stress.

The important thing to remember is that you are in control of your nightmares. All the unsettling images you see are merely the product of your own mind. Your inner self does not mean you any harm – in fact, it wants the best for you.

SWEET DREAMS ARE MADE OF THIS:

1. Go to bed on time. Steer clear of spooky movies, books, computer games and magazines.

2. Avoid cola or spicy food near bedtime. Drinks with caffeine stimulate your brain and the intense flavors of a late meal might keep you awake with indigestion.

3. Keep a friendly nightlight in your room, or try playing soothing music as you drift off to sleep.

4. Think positive thoughts as you shut your eyes. Try to re-live the nicest thing that happened that day.

5. If you do have a nightmare, settle yourself back to sleep by picturing yourself somewhere safe, such as on a beach or in a sunny garden.

6. In the morning, use your interpretation skills to analyze what the message of your nightmare could be.

7. If your bad dreams persist, talk to an adult you trust to find out about more ways for dealing with them.

Dreams of death

Every once in a while you might be unlucky enough to wake up with a horrible feeling in the pit of your stomach. There is nothing more disturbing than having to go through a nightmare in which somebody dies. These experiences can seem so graphic and real, you wake up convinced that something dreadful is sure to happen.

Back to reality

The good news is that it won't. Death dreams are symbolic and usually allude to a part of you that has now been replaced or taken away. When you move schools or start to take on a more grown-up role in your family, this new "life" can be marked by nightmares of this kind.

Learning to accept that this is your subconscious' way of dealing with the change will help you to let go and move forward. Although they might be terrifying at the time, dreams about death can even be positive experiences. If you learn how to understand their meaning, you'll see that they can simply indicate the end of one phase in your life and the start of another.

DREAMER'S REAL-LIFE ACCOUNT:

"I haven't had many nightmares, but there is one that stands out from the rest. Even thinking about this dream makes me shiver and try to block it out from my mind's eye. In this particular nightmare I was shocked to discover that I had killed someone! The scenario seemed so realistic I ended up going into my mom and dad's room until I was able to calm down. The next day I had a chat with my teacher about the dream. She suggested that the death could have something to do with coming back to school after the summer vacation. I think I've changed a lot over the six week break and I've made some brilliant new friends. Perhaps I needed to have this nightmare to say goodbye to the younger me I've left behind."

Alisha

I f you're struggling to unlock the messages hidden in your dreams, this dictionary can help you get started. This section of the book is a special glossary featuring the most common dream themes, plus ideas about what these symbols could signify. Among the A to Z entries in this section you'll also find some extra pages focusing on the images and issues that seem to crop up most in our sleeping lives.

When it comes to reading dreams, these pages don't hold all the answers. It's up to you to think through each possible meaning and then place it in the context of your own life and experiences. It's like trying on shoes until you find the pair that fits! Once you have discovered the interpretation that feels right, you'll be ready to create your own dreamer's dictionary – a personal handbook that is unique to you.

ACADEMY If you picture an academy or institution, there is a strong likelihood that an exciting prospect is waiting just around the corner. This opportunity may not involve learning or success – it could signal a new friendship instead.

ACCESSORIES When you adorn yourself with rings, bangles and other accessories, your inner self is implying that you are searching for something. Have a think about what might be missing – is it time to make up with a friend or find a new pastime?

ACCIDENT Don't be frightened by accident dreams, they are nearly always symbolic. Your inner self often uses these striking images to get you to slow down or take things a bit more carefully in your waking life.

ACTOR Acting can point to two very different meanings. While some dreamers are yearning to step into the spotlight, others are hiding behind a mask. If you secretly believe you are putting on an act, this dream should give you the courage to be yourself.

AIRPLANE Is your plane landing or taking off?
A departure can suggest a sudden journey into the
unknown, while a landing confirms the success of a
recent project. Air travel indicates that you are rising
above the norm. Think how this might apply to you.

ALIEN Have you come across something strange that
needs to be explored? Chances are that an alien can
symbolize an unfamiliar side of your character that
is coming to the surface.

ANGEL When angels appear in dreams, your inner self
is trying to soothe and comfort you. If you feel that
you need someone to look after you right now,
remember the deep connection you have with your
closest family and friends.

ARCADE Amusement arcades and funfairs suggest that
you've been messing around a lot recently. Only you
can decide whether it's time to stop now or enjoy the
fun while it lasts.

AUDIENCE Does it feel like the world is paying close
attention to your every move? If you have a big
decision coming up, take care to think it through
slowly and carefully.

Animals

Animals are one of the most common symbols to appear in dreams. At first their appearance can seem puzzling or just plain freaky! When you've got a science test on the brain, why on earth would your sleeping self conjure up creepy images of rats or a line of marching elephants? It's not until you make the connection between the emotion the animal represents and the events in your dream, that some meaning begins to fall into place.

Animals tend to represent a fundamental instinct deep within ourselves. Use the creature crib sheet opposite as a starting point, then think about how each animal's natural attributes might apply to your dream.

Alligator – cold-heartedness, danger
Bear – parent figure, sleep and hibernation
Bird – freedom, escape
Cat – magic and intuition
Cow – the female
Dog – faithfulness, friendship
Dolphin – companionship
Donkey – stubbornness
Elephant – patience, memory
Fish – feelings under the surface
Fox – cunning, slyness
Frog – transformation
Goat – a constant survivor
Horse – majesty and strength
Kangaroo – motherhood
Lion – courage, authority
Lizard – single-mindedness
Monkey – childishness, immaturity
Mouse – shyness
Owl – wisdom
Rat – anxiety, fear
Snake – disloyalty, trickery
Tortoise – slow progress
Wolf – power in numbers
Zebra – authority, balance

B

BABY Babies often symbolize the start of something. If you can't see any major changes on the horizon, it's time to look to yourself. Perhaps you need to protect a part of you that is helpless and innocent?

BAREFOOT Encounters in bare feet often suggest that you are happy and relaxed in your own skin. If your dream shows you searching for shoes, however, you should consider whether you have been behaving in a way that is unacceptable to those around you.

BELL If you are expecting some major news, this excitement could manifest itself in the form of a bell or alarm. Bells can also appear when your inner self is trying to warn you about something ahead.

BIRTHDAY CAKE Yum yum! A birthday cake is often a pat on the back for someone who is happy to share with the people around them. See this dream as a sign of the sweet things in your life.

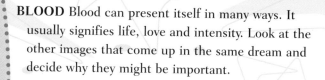

BLOOD Blood can present itself in many ways. It usually signifies life, love and intensity. Look at the other images that come up in the same dream and decide why they might be important.

BOOK Books and libraries are the essence of knowledge and learning. Take care to remember the title and the cover of any book you dream – they could direct you to new subjects and career plans.

BOY Are you so obsessed by your crush that he's even made it into your dream life? If the answer is a definite "no" then your subconscious could be hinting that you are searching for love.

BRIDGE Bridges feature in countless dreams. When you next cross one, ask yourself how you might be moving from one phase to another in life. A bridge can also symbolize a connection with someone special.

BUBBLE On first awakening, bubbles seem to sum up everything that is fun in life. They burst quickly, however, so think carefully about whether you have wishes that are unrealistic or fragile.

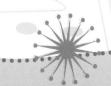

CAGE Whether it's at home, at school or with your friends, a part of you feels trapped. If the cage has a fierce creature pent up inside it, this might be a warning to keep your own wild side under control.

CASTLE Castles usually feature in positive dreams, signifying wealth and success. This may not seem to tally with your experiences at the moment. But keep an open mind – who knows what's coming your way?

CELEBRITY If you imagine yourself as a celebrity in your dream, it might be time to start planning the best way to really achieve your goals in life. If the celebrity in your dream is a friend, beware of putting him or her on a pedestal.

CELLPHONE Cellphones can indicate both good and bad communication. The person on the other end of the line is important – think how you relate to them and if there is anything special you need to say.

CHOCOLATE Dining out on chocolate might well indicate that you deserve a little luxury. Perhaps it's the reward for working hard or maybe something special after a long time without any treats?

CLOCK It doesn't take a genius to spot that clocks have a close connection with time. How this theme applies to you can be more difficult to figure out. Are you dealing with a deadline or do you need to make more time for someone or something?

CLOSET A large closet suggests transformation and change. What happens when you open the door and see what's lying inside?

CLOUD When you dream of clouds, it suggests that a part of your life might be foggy or confused. Are the clouds fluffy or stormy? Take a close look at the type of weather before drawing any conclusions.

CLOWN Jesters and clowns are your subconscious's way of telling you not to take life too seriously. Clowns show that it's okay to have fun and be silly from time to time.

COBWEB Is there something you need to brush away in your life? Cobwebs suggest that something is holding you back. Once you've made up your mind to get rid of the obstacle, things should improve.

DAGGER Do you sense that someone around you isn't being entirely honest? Ask yourself whether you're being deceived in some way, and then think through how to deal with it in a positive way.

DAISY Daisies and daisy chains often draw your mind back to the innocence of early childhood. Are you yearning for simpler times? It could also be a reminder that there's no need to feel guilty about something.

DANCING The interpretation of this dream rests on the sort of dance you are experiencing. A close dance with a partner shows that you are in sync with somebody special – a change of partners suggests one of you is moving on.

DENTIST Trips to the dentist aren't always pleasant, but they are good for you. This dream suggests that whatever you are experiencing is worth it, so the advice is to stick with things, if you can.

DESERT Are you feeling lonely at the moment? If you are, this might be manifested by a desert dream. Make the most of this time to get to know yourself – the situation won't last forever.

DIAMOND Diamonds are a girl's best friend, right? As well as being exquisitely beautiful, these gems might symbolize a request from your inner self to look at things clearly, accepting that there could be many sides to a situation.

DIARY Did the contents of the journal seem familiar, or did they bear no resemblance to your waking life? A diary keeper could be trying to rewrite history, so it might be time to accept the truth about something.

DINNER Dreamers who see themselves sitting round a table sharing a meal are usually thinking about their social life. Examine how you behaved at the meal and then decide whether you see your friends as equals.

DOLL How well do you really know your inner self? Playing with a doll can suggest that one part of you is wooden and uncommunicative. Consider if there's a side of you that needs to be comforted and looked after.

DRESS Dresses and frocks often feature in wish fulfilment dreams. Wearing a gorgeous gown makes most girls feel beautiful and feminine – enjoy!

EARTH Images of the Earth suggest that you are taking a wide, global view about something – or that you should be. Ask yourself whether you're looking at the bigger picture regarding the situation you're in.

EMBARRASSMENT Cringeworthy dreams can suggest that you are feeling insecure about something. Make a constructive list of things you can do to help yourself feel better, and your confidence will improve.

ENEMY Enemies can symbolize both real people and parts of your personality that bug you – what changes can you make to like yourself better? If you do clash with someone, try your best to make up with them.

ESCALATOR Try to remember if you were traveling up or down the escalator. Moving up shows that you are working through emotional issues, while down could imply that something is being repressed.

EXPLOSION A physical explosion in a dream often refers to an emotional outburst that has rocked your day. If this doesn't directly reflect your experience, think about whether something could be building up without you realizing.

FACE When a face features in your dreams, your mind is trying to understand how you choose to present yourself to the outside world. Is the face your own, or could your subconscious be suggesting that the person you reveal to everyone else isn't quite the real you?

FACTORY Factories are traditionally old-fashioned places where the work is repetitive and hours are long. Perhaps you're ready to do something unpredictable – have a think about how you could be more creative.

FAILURE This dream doesn't usually suggest you are going to fail – it could be your mind working through a very natural and common fear. Face the feeling your dream gives you and then make plans for success.

FAIRY It looks as though your mind is searching for help from someone or something. If you've run out of solutions for a problem, it could be time to consider calling on some outside help.

FEATHER Feathers are very spiritual objects, often connected with our souls. If this doesn't seem to fit with your thoughts right now, the feather in your dreams could represent the need for a gentle attitude.

87

Family

If you flick back through your dream journal, who pops up the most? Most girls will find that their family are the people who join them again and again in their dreams. In many ways this isn't earth-shattering stuff – the people who we stare at across the dinner table and fight with over the TV remote are simply the ones we spend the most time with.

Dreams (or occasionally nightmares!) focusing on your family can often be very extreme. People shouting, hurting each other or storming out of the home are all fairly typical. The shocking nature of these dreams is deliberately created by your subconscious as a way of releasing your unexpressed feelings. It's like turning on a tap and letting all the bad stuff flood out in a safe and controlled way.

Family life can be rocky sometimes – nobody has the ability to wind us up more than our cheeky little brother, annoying older sister or our parents!

When you next have a dream about someone in your family, think carefully about your feelings towards them. Remember that a change in family set-up – perhaps due to parental separation or a new arrival – can increase the intensity of your feelings. Work through the five questions below and really probe why your inner self is presenting your family in this manner. Getting to know yourself in this way might help you to understand the people in your family better, too.

RELATIVE VALUES

1. Is the family member acting as normal?

2. Do I feel close to this person in my dream?

3. Does the same attitude, discussion or row get acted out again and again?

4. Have the family roles been mixed up in any way?

5. Is there something specific he or she is saying to me?

F ...

FIREWORK Dreams about fireworks generally indicate plans for success and celebration. Hopefully something spectacular is on the horizon! If you find the display scary, your inner self might also be feeling a teeny bit nervous about the future.

FLAG Have a good, long think – is your inner self trying so hard to get a message across that it has been forced to wave a flag under your nose?

FLOOD A raging flood might suggest that you are struggling to keep your head above water. If it feels as though your emotions are running wild at the moment, try to view this as a temporary situation that will pass.

FOG Dreams about fog can be mystifying. Rest assured that the clouds will lift, but at the moment your inner self is feeling confused and unsure of the best way forward. Help yourself move on by confronting any issues that need to be dealt with.

FOREST Walking through the dark paths of a forest may suggest that you are thinking very deeply about something or someone. Let your instincts guide you forward, just as they did in your dream.

FRIEND Observe your friends carefully when they appear in dreams. Their language and behavior can provide good pointers as to how your relationships are going, and how you fit in with your group.

FRUIT Have you done well recently in a competition or test? Fruit often symbolizes the just rewards due for a good job done. Give yourself a pat on the back, your inner self thinks you deserve it!

FUNERAL Dreams about funerals can be unsettling. As with any aspect of death, these dreams tend to be symbolic rather than literal. Funerals often signify the end of one situation and the start of something new.

FURNITURE Strangely enough, a collection of furniture in a room can represent how we feel about our family. Did the pieces go together well in your dream? Perhaps your mind is urging you to pull your folks together to bring about some positive changes.

Future

Focusing on your hopes for the future is both an exciting and positive thing to do. There is also evidence to suggest that, if used correctly, your subconscious can really help make your dreams come true!

Some dream experts believe that your inner self can link together details and facts, making connections that the waking part of your brain is too busy to process. This could explain why your dreaming mind sometimes knows what is coming before you do.

Our hopes and wishes for the future take up a large part of our attention, whether we're asleep or awake. The direction in which our life is heading is naturally very important to us all. If you experience a dream where the action is located in the future, your mind is playing out how your life might go if you select one particular option over another one.

1. Encourage wish fulfilment
Wish fantasies are extremely pleasurable, but they are often so far out of reach you could never imagine them happening for real. If you incubate a realistic and achievable dream, however, you might help your waking self move a bit closer toward it.

2. Get a goal
Instead of worrying about the future, set yourself a goal and then visualize it in your dreams. Imagine yourself on a road moving toward the goal — progress may be slow, but if you keep heading in the right direction the future you want could be yours.

3. Stay focused
We all want the moon and the stars, but if you focus your dreams on just a single desire, the energy you need to make it happen will be all the more intense.

4. Ignore the negatives
You deserve happiness and success just as much as the next person. There is no reason why good things shouldn't happen to you, so make a real effort to banish any doubts whenever they creep in. Positive people have a funny knack of getting into positive situations!

GAME SHOW Your inner self might use a TV format to suggest how you are doing in the game of life. Don't panic if you're not playing well – we also know that these shows aren't to be taken too seriously.

GARDEN To decipher this dream, you need to think carefully about how the garden is presented. A budding, flowering oasis suggests that you are a creative girl in full bloom; a weedy dry area implies you need to take care of yourself a bit more.

GATE Gates generally stand for change – the movement from one phase to the next. If the gate is blocked, ask yourself whether you're ready to move forward as quickly as you thought you were.

GHOST Seeing a ghost is a pretty freaky experience, but in your dreaming life they usually appear to remind you of something from the past. The ghost's identity and what it says should give you vital clues.

GIFT Everyone loves a gift, even a subconscious one! If you receive a present in your dream, consider its contents carefully. The gift could symbolize a talent or skill you never knew you had.

GLASS Even though you can see through glass, it is also incredibly tough. Are you building a barrier around yourself or are you finding it hard to get close to someone? Smashing glass suggests that you are breaking through at last.

GLOVE Gloves are a metaphor for the things we hide from the people around us. When you take your gloves off, your inner self is trying to show that you are being honest and respectful – how could this apply to your dream?

GODDESS Goddesses often make an appearance when you're experiencing a classic wish fulfilment dream. These lovely figures are your inner self's way of agreeing that it's great to be a girl sometimes!

GOLD Congratulations, it look as though you have come across something valuable! Remember, dreams can be symbolic rather than literal. Is there a friendship or some news you should be celebrating?

GRASS A lawn bursting with fresh green grass often represents an exciting new idea. If the grass in your dream is rather more patchy, you could be struggling to find a solution to a tricky problem.

HAIR Hair dreams challenge all your interpretation skills – the first step is to ask yourself how your hair was presented. Was it messy, straight or short? Are you untangling a problem, or even cutting away the past?

HAT As with most items of clothing, putting on a hat hints that you are trying to hide something or disguise the real you. If you can see how this is happening in your waking life, you'll see how to set things straight.

HILL If you are struggling up a hill, your inner self is recognizing all the hard work and effort you are putting into a project. If you are right at the top, it would seem that you have succeeded already.

HOME No matter how brave we are, every one of us needs to have a place where we feel loved and safe. Dreaming of home could mean that you feel relaxed or that you long for security in one area of your life.

ICE Ice is all about emotions. Are you freezing someone out without even realizing it? If this doesn't sound likely, you need to ask yourself whether you're the one being shut out in the cold.

ICE CREAM If you love ice cream (along with the rest of us!), this dream will leave you with a feeling of pleasure and happiness. On a deeper level, melting ice cream reminds us that nothing in life stays the same.

ILLNESS Don't be too obsessed by the illness you are dreaming about – instead question whether you are looking after yourself. Take steps to pamper yourself and you should feel better in your dreams as well.

INK Your school work may well be on your mind right now – ink in dreams often indicates increased knowledge. A spill of ink, however, could suggest a small problem that needs to be corrected during waking hours.

ISLAND Islands are beautiful, but lonely places. You need to decide whether being alone is your choice. Are you taking time to recharge your batteries or would it help to reach out to those around you?

JAILER Could the jailer in your dream actually be you? Only your inner self has the freedom to see when you are being restricted by an uptight part of your own personality. Although it's hard, try to break free from these insecurities.

JAW This image often appears in a nightmare. Graphic images such as snapping jaws are your inner self's way of shouting at the top of its voice. If you can work out why you are under attack, you'll be sure to stop it.

JEWELRY Personal bling isn't the least bit subtle – all that sparkle shows how you are feeling about yourself right now. Don't be ashamed of this pride, your inner self wants you to dazzle...

JIGSAW When your subconscious shows you a puzzle, it is asking you to hold off from making a decision. Double-check you have got all the facts first, and that all the key pieces are in place.

JUGGLING A juggler indicates you have got everything in balance, unless he or she is dropping balls all over the floor! Are you struggling with commitments? If so, this would be a good time to give something up.

K

KARAOKE Hijacking the mic to belt out your favorite tune might well happen in a wish fulfilment dream. If you're not a disco diva, your inner self could be trying to warn you from being a bit too big for your boots.

KETTLE Why is your inner self focusing on such an everyday object? Kettles are connected with the practical side of our personalities. Could there be a job or a task you are forgetting to do?

KEY Keys unlock doors, but occasionally they lock things up again, too. These powerful symbols represent new ideas, change and greater understanding of yourself. Study the context of your dream carefully – it's sure to be loaded with clues.

KID Growing up is exciting, but the child inside us is always there somewhere. If you present yourself as a kid in your dreams, your inner self might be telling you not to be embarrassed about this innocent side.

KNITTING Unless the wool is unravelling, knitting is a happy motif suggesting that things are coming together for you. Your inner self is thrilled with the achievement, so you should be proud, too.

Love

As you move through your teens, your dreaming mind may spend many nights working through your relationships and devising strategies to win love. Everyone's heart yearns for companionship – in fact, the status of your love life has a huge influence over your happiness and health.
If you haven't had a relationship yet, or you aren't in one right now, your subconscious will be there each night to help you sort through your feelings.

Romantic dreams can be extremely profound and even unsettling. Sometimes your inner self will matchmake you with the most unlikely, unsuitable people or roleplay shocking breakup scenes. Other wish fulfilment dreams are so emotionally captivating, you feel disappointed when you wake up to find they were just a dream.

Even though these dreams are both personal and intense, normal rules apply when it comes to interpreting what they mean to you. Put any angry, guilty or tearful feelings aside and look honestly at the symbols and context of the experience. Use the skills you gained in the earlier chapters to read each insightful message and then move on.

I LOVE DREAMS!

1. Don't feel guilty about your relationship dreams — remember they usually aren't literal.

2. Can you pick up any tips from the relationships you observe in your dreams? Is your inner self trying to point out someone who deserves your attention or could it be showing you another way of handling a certain situation?

3. Don't get too preoccupied with the random people who pop up in your dreams. There's more to be learnt from studying the conversations and relationships at play.

4. Trust your heart. If you don't understand what your dream is trying to tell you right now, the truth will present itself in time.

LADDER Ladders become magical symbols when they appear in dreamscapes, just like gates and doorways. The biggest clue to interpreting their meaning is to work out whether you are climbing up or down.

LAUGHING If you dream of laughing, your inner self thinks it's time to give yourself a break. A giggle with your girlfriends will be a dose of the perfect medicine.

LAUNDRY Are you trying to change your image? Washing clothes suggests you are trying to scrub up for someone special. It's good to take pride in your appearance, but make sure that all this effort is what you really want.

LEGS A dream that focuses on your legs makes it clear that you are standing on your own two feet, or that you ought to start. Think about how independent you are and you'll soon see how this dream relates to you.

LETTER A letter is a clear message from your subconscious, but you'll have to open it before you can decode its meaning. Look at the handwriting, contents and who the letter is from before coming to a conclusion.

MAGAZINE Flicking through a glossy magazine hints that you are open to new ideas. The cover, title, headlines and photos should give you a feel for the issue to which your mind is referring.

MAKE-UP Very heavily applied make-up has a similar meaning to a mask. Are you proud of your image, or hiding behind a personality that isn't really you at all? Have the courage to let your inner beauty shine.

MAP Be prepared: change could be waiting just around the corner! A map signifies a brand new direction for you, whether that's in school, in your relationships or the start of an exciting new hobby.

MIRROR Mirror sequences suggest that you are thinking hard about your inner self. Decide whether you are happy with the reflection you see and you'll get a good idea of your current confidence levels.

Money

It's pretty hard to find a girl who couldn't do with a bit more money in her wallet these days! When you come across cash in your dream life, however, your subconscious is referring to all the things you need.

Money metaphors

• *Being broke*

When you are hard-up in your dreams, it would seem that you are feeling low in confidence. Are your friends turning their backs on you, or making you feel unimportant? Being short of money might reflect feelings of low status. Think why you are feeling like this and figure out ways to make the situation better.

• *Finding cash*

Digging up treasure or finding money in the street suggests that you are looking for something that is important to you. This could be a new possession, a friend or acceptance from others.

● *Losing money*
Have you suffered a blow recently in some area of
your life? When money slips through your fingers,
your subconscious might be referring to a wasted
opportunity or a setback that is troubling you.
Again, your confidence might be dipping, so try to
find positive ways to build yourself back up.

● *Giving money away*
The interpretation of this dream depends on who is
doing the giving! If you are the generous one, it
would seem that you are being especially loving and
kind to those around you, or that you have good
feelings for someone. To watch another person hand
out cash suggests that they aren't giving you their
time and attention.

Dreams are unfettered by the demands of our
throwaway, hundred-mile-an-hour society.
Although you think money is important to
you, you will need to look deeper at your inner
self to find out what really matters.

M ...

MONK The figure of a monk can be creepy, but the image is often used to show that you are thinking very deeply about life. Monks are associated with the spiritual and religious sides of your personality.

MONSTER Nightmares are filled with all kinds of terrifying creatures. The worst are the beasts that won't fully reveal themselves. Try really hard to face up to the things that are worrying you and the monsters should run away.

MONUMENT A large monument presents all the things you are proud of. A statue or plaque suggests you'd like other people to recognize these achievements and remember that they belong to you.

MOON The moon is an intensely female image. It seems as though you are in touch with your mysterious side and using your intuition just as your inner self would like you to.

MORNING A bright sunrise or a breakfast scene are clear heralds of a new beginning. Very rarely, however, a morning dream can be prompted by a pun on the word "mourning."

MOSAIC Mosaics are complex images made up of thousands of tiny parts, just like our own lives. If there's something on your mind, it really can help to step back and observe the bigger picture.

MOVIE Generally when you watch a movie in your dream, your subconscious is trying hard to make sense of your behavior. Try to recall the movie's storyline then see if you can draw any learning points from it.

MUD Mud crops up when you're feeling bogged down by a situation. Pulling yourself out of it might be difficult, but your inner self is encouraging you to try your best to clean away the stuff and nonsense that is making you feel bad.

MUSEUM Museums can be seen as dusty places devoted to history. Perhaps you're being a little old-fashioned about an issue? Otherwise your subconscious could be trying to learn something new from the past.

MUSIC Music represents the link between our waking and sleeping selves. If the harmonies in your dream are sweet and melodic, it suggests that you are a well-rounded person who is in tune with her inner self.

N

NAILS Long fingernails might be your inner self trying to prove that you've got what it takes to hold on to something important. If you break a nail, it's time to stop stressing about the details in life.

NECKLACE A beautiful necklace hides a desire to have power over those around you. Do you wear statement jewelry in this way, or could it be something you secretly dream of?

NEEDLE Something needs mending in your life, but what could it be? A falling out with a friend, a thoughtless word or something as simple as a broken object might be in need of your attention.

NIGHT Scenes after dark make it obvious that there are things you are grappling with that aren't entirely clear. Talking about your worries is the best way of bringing them into the light.

NUMBER Figures often have a personal meaning, based around the dates that mean the most to you. Consider each number and then think what birthdays, ages and anniversaries they might relate to.

OCEAN Most watery dreams relate to the swirling nature of our emotions. Traveling across the ocean shows that you are brave, while a calm sea suggests that your inner self is at peace with the world.

OFFICE Even though you may be too young to work fulltime, offices often pop up in teen dreams. Are you working efficiently on a project, or is your inner self trying to nudge you into getting more organized?

OPERATION Surgery can suggest that you've got a persistent worry on your mind. Try to pinpoint if there is something specific you need to get out of your system and then help yourself to move on.

ORCHESTRA A finely tuned orchestra makes a lovely, soothing sound. When one pops up in your dreams, lie back and enjoy the music – both your waking and sleeping lives are clearly in harmony.

OVEN Ovens and baking refer to an ability to cook something lovely out of a few basic ingredients. Maybe you've brought your friends together in a fun way or done something to make your family smile?

PAPER A blank sheet may expose a need to talk, while a drawing can indicate that it's time to start expressing yourself better. Consider trying to improve channels of communication with those closest to you.

PARCEL Packages represent experiences that we have yet to explore and fully understand. Think about the gift and its contents carefully, then ask yourself how they might relate to your daily life.

PARTY Party dreams can often unveil a desire to be more sociable or to truly belong in your crowd of friends. Look at ways of boosting your confidence, perhaps by joining a club or meeting new people.

PASSENGER Do you feel in control of your destiny? Being a passenger could suggest that you have a need to get in the driving seat for a change! If there are some big decisions ahead of you, work out how to put yourself in charge.

PASSWORD Do you sense that the path is blocked or maybe you're feeling a little pushed out in one aspect of your life? Concentrate on re-experiencing your dream and the emotional jam might be eased.

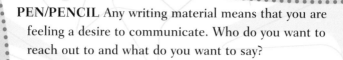
PEN/PENCIL Any writing material means that you are feeling a desire to communicate. Who do you want to reach out to and what do you want to say?

PERFUME A familiar scent is our mind recalling a very specific person or experience that means a lot to us. Who or what do you think it could be? It could just be a great memory that you should enjoy!

PHOTOGRAPH A photograph means that you are looking in on yourself. Assess the picture in your dream, focusing on where and when it was taken.

PIANO Even if you can't see it right now, everything is coming together for you. If you are having a tough time, things will get better. A piano symbolizes harmony – are you in tune with someone special?

PIG Are you or someone close to you being a little selfish about something? Take a hard look at yourself and those around you to find out why this behavior might be troubling you.

PURSE When you dream, your subconscious often uses a purse to represent the responsibilities we each carry around with us. Study the purse's contents – it could contain all manner of important symbols.

QUARREL In our dreams we can fall out with the people we least expect to clash with. Search your mind to discover why you have these bad feelings. Are you angry with that person or it is you who is to blame?

QUEEN If you see yourself on the throne, you are feeling very much in control of a certain situation. If another person is the queen, your inner self might be putting her forward as someone you can turn to for advice.

QUEUE All queuers will know that good things are worth the wait. We all need to be more patient from time to time, so give things a chance before tearing off and leaving others behind.

QUICKSAND Somewhere deep inside you are feeling insecure and helpless. Although very few of us will ever see real quicksand, this image immediately conjures up images of being trapped. Accepting these fears is your first step towards finding solid ground.

QUIZ Even though quizzes are just for fun, you seem to be scared of making a fool of yourself. Instead of worrying about failure, concentrate on all the good things that new challenges bring.

RACE Races are associated with measuring your progress. Are you flying ahead or do you feel you're lagging behind all your friends? If you can forget the rest and focus on yourself, the race pressure will automatically disappear.

RADIO When your dream self listens to the radio, take care to remember what's being played. The programme, DJ and music could all offer vital clues about the people you're most tuned into.

RAINBOW A multicolored rainbow is a sign of hope. Sometimes the symbol comes after a difficult time, helping your subconscious to reassure you that better days are ahead. Each of the rainbow colors has its own meaning:

- Red – strength, energy and power
- Orange – happiness and independence
- Yellow – transparency and honesty
- Green – harmony and balance
- Blue – healing and rest
- Indigo – spirituality
- Violet – respect and peace

R ...

RECIPE It seems that this is an especially creative time for you. Recipes symbolize the many talents that we each possess – if you don't feel like a fount of good ideas yet, you should do shortly.

REHEARSAL Your inner self is preparing you for something emotional you need to face in waking life. A rehearsal dream can be a way of taking a dry run at something that is going to be difficult to say.

RESTAURANT When your sleeping soul visits cafés and restaurants, it is seeking out company. If it feels as though your friends aren't really there for you at the moment, maybe it's time to look outside the crowd for someone new to talk to.

RIBBON Ribbons are pretty, frivolous things. If you come across braid in the course of your dreams, your inner self could be trying to highlight something or someone who is shallow or superficial.

RING A ring is inserted into a dream in place of an important relationship. Look at the circumstances to see whether the ring symbolizes a person you know or a different part of your own personality.

RIVER Rivers are usually calming, but they can also suggest you are not in control of your own destiny. If you think you are drifting through life, reconsider recent decisions to make sure that they are really right for you.

ROAD Roads take us from one point to another. What have you got coming up in the future? A bumpy ride or a smooth straight road will give you a sense of how the journey might pan out.

ROBOT Is it time to put some heart and soul into an area of your life? Robots suggest that you are simply going through the motions in a mindless and mechanical way. Consider honestly why this is happening, as it could be for self-protection.

ROLLER COASTER You are probably going through some intense highs and lows in a relationship. Roller coasters suggest stormy times, so it's best to hold on until the ride is over.

ROPE Rope dreams can be loaded with metaphors and puns that hint at what your heart is trying say. Have you been roped into something, or is a situation tying you down? Study the context, and the message should become clear.

School

You have to be there over 30 hours a week, so it's no wonder that school can play a big part in both your waking and sleeping life. Schools are usually the venue for the classic anxiety dream of failing a test or exam.

School of thought

If you're having a rough time at school, this turmoil will surface in your dream life again and again until it gets resolved. A scary teacher, difficult homework or bullies can all make it very tricky for you to switch off at the end of the day.

If problems don't seem to be working themselves out, write down all the ways you could try to deal with them. When you go to bed each night, take the time to think through all these positive thoughts and see if you can incubate some dreams to help the situation.

$2 + 2 = 4$

If your tactics don't seem to be working, it's time to talk to your parents or a friendly adult who can help. You'll be able to tell by now that, as with all these subconscious scenarios, school dreams symbolize emotions and attitudes rather than things that will literally happen.

When classrooms crop up in your sleep, it usually suggests that there is something you need to learn. This could be a practical thing, such as your French vocab, or a much more significant life-skill or lesson that involves your friends, family or relationships.

Look at the context of the dream, the dialogue and the people who feature in it to try to uncover what your subconscious is attempting to tell you.

Look at school motifs that crop up in other dreams, too. Unexpected entrances from teachers, school books and long-forgotten pupils from your school will all have some kind of significance and can show you where your life is right now.

SANDWICH When you dream about something as small as a sandwich, there is often a specific hidden message. Sandwiches suggest you are feeling under pressure or stuck in middle of something.

SCISSORS When your subconscious believes you need to cut yourself free from a person or a situation, scissors will appear in your dreams. Think things over carefully before you decide the best move to make.

SHOES Focus on the style and color of the shoes – they could give you vital clues about your personality. Shoes also represent your approach to life, so check to see whether the pair fits and is suitable for you.

SNOW When an idea is coming together, you might be lucky enough to experience a snowy dream. Although snow is cold, your inner self is also showing you that it represents the crystallization of something beautiful.

SPACE Space dreams are there to show you the vastness of your own potential. If you are feeling rather small at the moment, take courage and think about all the amazing things you can do.

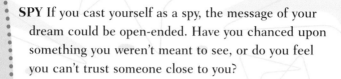

SPY If you cast yourself as a spy, the message of your dream could be open-ended. Have you chanced upon something you weren't meant to see, or do you feel you can't trust someone close to you?

STAR Stars twinkle in the night sky and on the stage and screen. Whichever kind you dream of, it seems you are hoping to get noticed. Keep believing in yourself and you will sparkle just as brightly.

STRANGER Mysterious figures are unsettling because they symbolize an element of your personality that doesn't normally surface during waking hours. You could be ready to recognize a part of you that is normally repressed.

SUNGLASSES Shades are a very direct way of telling you that you aren't seeing things as clearly as you should. Try your best to stop focusing on the negative, and everything will be so much brighter.

SWING It looks as though you're agonizing over some kind of decision. Going back and forth on a swing is a physical manifestation of your mind sizing up pros and cons. Relive the dream, follow your heart and then pick the option that feels right.

TEDDY BEAR Teddy bears symbolize security, but they also suggest the world of small children. Take a look at your closest relationships and think about your behavior. Are you being a teensy bit immature?

TEXT MESSAGE Texts, instant messaging and email show how effectively we connect with our friends. Study the content of your texts and you should get a grasp on how well your friendships are going.

THIEF Picturing yourself as a thief does not mean you are a bad person. This type of dream suggests that you are worried about losing something which belongs to you, or are feeling unworthy.

THUNDER The rumble of thunder can be a warning from your subconscious. It seems that there is a storm brewing, so think things through before you erupt into an outburst you might later regret.

TOES Toes and feet symbolize the direction you are taking in life and how you are progressing. Are you happy or should you make changes? It could be time to turn your attention to the little things in life.

TOWER The view from a tower suggests that you have set yourself high expectations. Check that the tower has a door, however – if the entrance is missing you might be out of touch with your inner self.

TOYS Toys remind us of little brothers and sisters, but they also represent the creative part of our own spirits. If toys regularly feature in your dreams, your subconscious is telling you not to hide your playful side.

TRAIN When a train rumbles through your dream, your inner self is insinuating that you are conforming with the rest of the crowd. This is no bad thing necessarily, but it's helpful to be aware of it.

TUNNEL Traveling through a gloomy tunnel can symbolize exploration and discovery. Look back and decide whether you have learnt something new about yourself recently, so that you can keep moving forward.

TWINS If you don't know the twins in your dream, these characters can represent two sides of the same idea. Are the twins friends or foes? We often come up against conflicts, but a twin dream might just help us work them out.

UFO If you spot a UFO in your dreams, you could be searching to discover more about yourself. Flying saucers are associated with the unknown, so perhaps you are trying to push the boundaries in your life.

UMBRELLA We open an umbrella when we need shelter and protection. Look at the dream and see whether you can pinpoint if there is someone who might be ready to offer you the support you need.

UNDERWATER If you dive into water in your dream, it could suggest that your emotions are getting on top of you. Underwater dreams suggest that you are feeling out of control: take a deep breath and think what you can do to change this.

UNICORN These magical beasts stand for strong principles and a sense of duty. If you see a white unicorn, your inner self is grappling especially hard to choose the right thing to do in your waking life.

UNICYCLE If you can manage to ride a unicycle in your dreams, you should give yourself a pat on the back! It seems as though you are in control of everything you do and say.

VACATION Even your dream self needs a vacation every so often! This is a common night theme when you are in need of a break from the grind of school and homework. Make time to give yourself a rest.

VALLEY Traveling into a deep valley is another metaphor for the journey into your subconscious. Your sleeping self is digging through your most personal thoughts in order to really understand itself.

VEGETABLE Potatoes, carrots and greens suggest your subconscious is hungering for something that will do you good. Do you need a friendly ear to listen to you?

VEIL A veil suggests a secret. Think about your friends and family – is someone hiding something?

VIDEO CAMERA If you are trying to video your dreams, it suggests you need to look at a situation objectively. Keep your emotions in check and you may be able to see things as they really are.

VOLCANO If your hidden emotions are bubbling up inside you, beware – when they erupt it could be explosive for everyone concerned.

WAIST Did you know that an ample waist in your dreams rarely means you are overweight? Instead your subconscious uses this symbol to suggest that you are content and enjoying life.

WAITRESS Even the most pleasant dreams featuring waitresses can say a lot about how you prioritize your time. Try not to spend too much time caring for everybody else – it's easy to forget you have needs, too.

WALLET You may have found something of value, although it is probably not financial. To lose a wallet in your dreams could also suggest that you are letting go of something important. Is this accidental?

WAND Each wave of a magic wand suggests that you have a spellbinding influence over the people around you. If someone uses a wand to control you, be wary of this person in your waking life.

WATERFALL A glistening waterfall indicates that you are letting go of something, possibly in a spectacular fashion. Take a look at how you've felt recently. Perhaps you need to release some pent-up emotion?

WHEELBARROW Trundling a wheelbarrow around any kind of outdoor space can reveal the amount of hard work and energy you are putting into something. Is a distraction taking up too much time or is the project truly worthwhile?

WHISPER When we hear whispers our inner self is trying to coax us to listen more carefully to what is going on around us. Whispered voices only pass on a few of the facts, so you'll need to focus to find out more.

WINDOW Usually, windows offer you a broad perspective on the outside world. If you are on the brink of making a decision, your inner self may show you a window to give you a sense of all the possibilities ahead of you.

WING If you sprout wings in your dream, you're probably on course for a very uplifting experience! Angels have wings to help them soar above the ground – perhaps you need to rise above things, too.

WITCH Witches aren't necessarily evil, it all depends on the form they take in your dreams. A wicked, cackling witch often alludes to a part of yourself you don't like. Try to change this for the better and the witches should fly away.

X The letter X in a dream is "marking the spot" or signposting something that needs your special attention. It can also hint at a mistake that might have happened, either at home or at school.

X-RAY A hospital scene showing an X-ray suggests that you feel the need to delve below the surface. Can you see through someone who is bugging you, or are you the one who needs to be analyzed?

XYLOPHONE A tinkly musical instrument like a xylophone might foretell an upcoming change. If you play with ease, the transition could be straightforward.

YACHT For most of us, a luxury yacht is a world away from our everyday lives. This might be a simple wish fulfilment dream or a more general desire for wealth.

YAWN You're asleep when you dream, but if you are still yawning in this super-relaxed state you are definitely bored in some way! Take a look at your free time and see if you can find an exciting new activity to take up.

YELL Shouting is always distressing, even in your dreams. This may be a processing dream where you are trying to make sense of an upsetting exchange that took place earlier. If not, think hard about what could be making you angry inside.

YETI If an abominable snowman features in your dream life, your inner self could be thinking about the unknown world. Yetis who give chase symbolize the need to explore your mystical side.

ZODIAC Are you the sort of girl who loves to check her stars? Astrology dreams are closely bound up with the personalities of the twelve signs. Your inner self might use these symbols to direct your thoughts toward someone special.

ZOO These dreams depend heavily on the way in which the zoo is presented and arranged. Is everyone having fun, or do the animals seem trapped in their cages? The puns and metaphors will lead you to the answers.

Good luck and sweet dreams!